£2

# Solitaire

First Published 2007 by Templar Poetry
Templar Poetry is an imprint of Delamide & Bell

Templar Poetry
Fenelon House
Kingsbridge Terrace
58 Dale Road, Matlock, Derbyshire
DE4 3NB

ISBN-13 978-1-906285-04-3

Typeset by Pliny
Graphics by Paloma Violet
Printed and bound in India

*Templar Poetry Pamphlets*
*2007*

## WAVE
*Pat Borthwick*

## TEST PAPER
*Linda Cash*

## DREAMING OF WALLS
## REPEATING THEMSELVES
*Pat Winslow*

*Templar Poetry Pamphlets*
*2006*

## PILLARS OF SALT
*Judy Brown*

## WAITING TO BURN
*Angela Cleland*

## SOME HISTORIES OF THE SHEFFIELD FLOOD 1864
*Rob Hindle*

## ALICE
*Jane Weir*

**www.templarpoetry.co.uk**

# Acknowledgements

Several of these poems have been published previously in a number of magazines including *Ambit.*, 'The Summer My Father Died' by Mara Bergman. Both of Stephen Wilson's poems, 'Welsh-English Dictionary' and 'Anniversary', were first published in *Magma 34 &37* respectively and 'Welsh-Engish Dictionary has also been published on the South Bank Online Poetry Library. 'The Look' and 'Getting His Head Straight' by Derek Adams were first published in *Obsessed With Pipework (2005)* and *Magma 28* respectively. Dawn Wood's poem 'Comparison of a Black Labrador with a Sikka Deer Skull' was published in *PN Review 162 (2005)*

Acknowledgments are due to all the writers who submitted their work. Thanks are due to Jean Sprackland who was the Judge for the competition and the anthology.

Templar Poetry also acknowledges widespread support from many individuals and organisations throughout the British Isles, Ireland and beyond who publicised the competition. The work of Templar Poetry is facilitated by support provided by Arts Council England.

# Foreword

The Annual Templar Poetry Pamphlet & Collection Competition provides contemporary poets with an opportunity to have their work published in pamphlet, anthology and collection form. The three overall winners each have their submission published as an individual pamphlet and the opportunity to publish more of their work as a full collection. A selection of the best individual poems from the remaining submissions are published in this anthology.

The three pamphlets and the anthology are launched at the Derwent Poetry Festival in Derbyshire, staged during a late autumn weekend each year, in one of Richard Arkwright s former mills in the spectacular Derwent Gorge. The Pamphlet & Collection Competition Awards is the opening event of the Festival and showcases readings from the pamphlet competition winners, anthology poets and other Templar Poetry writers.

New collections are launched over the festival weekend from both Templar Poetry and other publishers, and the festival is rounded off with a reading by a guest poet.

Templar Poetry is committed to publishing excellent contemporary poetry, and to developing and widening the readership and audience for new poets and new poetry. Further information about Templar Poetry and its work is posted on our website where full details of our list can be viewed, and our poetry can also be purchased online. Our books are also available from good booksellers.

www.templarpoetry.co.uk

# Contents

# Getting his Head Straight

The construction took a week
of his spare time, more or less,
and that included queuing
at the checkout, for the wood,
sashcord, pulley and two breeze blocks.
The steel came from a scrap yard,
quite cheap, but he had to grind
the edge himself.
All day Sunday experimenting
with the release, the drop,
smoothing and waxing the runners.
Four cabbages and finally
a leg of pork. Afterwards
he cooked one half of the meat,
threw the other away.

For three and half weeks
it has stood there, in the bedroom.
Every night before turning off the light,
he has looked at it and smiled.

Tonight is the night, he has decided,
a large glass of Talisker,
a bath, some candles, the CD player on,
Roberta Flack is singing
'The first time ever I saw your face'.
He is lying, face down, naked,
still slightly damp, smelling of Radox,
cord in his right hand,
trying to get his head straight,
waiting for the track to end.

## The Look

"You're right, you don't
forget a thing like that"
he turned the apple slowly
studied the uneven furrows his
teeth had made, the
slight brown bruising
on the white flesh,
held it up close to his eye, stared
into a dark round hole, wondered
what had made it and
if it was still in the apple or
if it had departed
or if - he swallowed -
it was too late to worry.
"I remember my first time, the
look on his face, not surprise,
it was as if he'd just thought of
something important to say"

## Getting Away

It's not the sort of place we'd normally go.
But it was cheap and all there was.
From the balcony you looked out over the sea
which we were told was once azure blue
and sparkled like a net of daimonds.
The hills behind used to provide habitats
for three rare species of parrot
and a bark-eating mammal the local cuisine
was famous for. The town itself was soporific,
the inhabitants like sleep-walkers, eyes open
but fixed on a make-believe horizon.
At night all the men disappeared.
The women dressed in black.
The children of course pestered you,
standing where the tourist sights had been,
holding their hands out shouting
*photograph, photograph.*
None of the pictures have come out.

## The Summit

We set off single file above a tideline of oil and dead gannets,
a sharp light bleeding where sky and ocean collided.

The place was a crumbling bungalow, some old-timer's
holiday haunt, walls now pocked by shrapnel and bullets.

He came out to meet us, all smile and guile, shook hands with his left,
held up his right to display the stub of thumb and index.

A gift, he said, to God, then steered me inside. The cut of his suit
was sharp as a cutlass, his taste in ties garish.

Two lumpy chairs, rum in black tea brewed on a primus,
a driftwood fire and local radio floating through from the kitchen

where our aides sat it out playing blackjack for matchsticks.
His quick boyish giggle, the bone of a smile in my throat.

A bad joke we both laughed at too loud. Then it was business:
exits bolted and sealed, armed guards round the back;

the cut and the deal, not playing it too close to your chest,
not showing your hand; the saving of face by risking your neck.

## Keys

There are five of them. They hang
from their chain like the fingers
of a smashed hand,
divining bones.

They open gates, heavy-hinged doors,
or lock the day down,
slammed answer
to a question out of place.

The long chain swings from my waist.
I'm a key-slave shackled to their spell.
Nagged by gravity
they wear my pocket thin.

Sometimes I'll reach a gate to hoik out
a mesh of metal wands in a knot
of links I have to shake free
like a shaman's rattle.

Beyond the bars a shadow in a recess shifts.
Let us through boss?
A dash, a skirl of dust,
a sparrow on the gym roof.

## Unspecified Crimes

I knew him immediately from the way he looked
just like everyone else, from the way his eyes
stared somewhere beyond me, from the way a brief
anaesthesia came over me as I passed him.

It was rush hour. I turned. He was easy to follow,
not hurrying or dawdling. A man who knew
his place in the day, in his briefcase an empty lunchbox,
a holiday brochure, a few unfinished accounts.

Outside the tube he stood for a smoke, long drags
as if it were fresh air. A tug at cuff-linked cuffs, fingers
adjusting the knot of his tie like a pre-arranged sign
and he slipped underground. The Circle line, anti-clockwise,

to emerge ten stops later, take a maze of rights and lefts
like a man with a ball of string for a brain and a home
in one of those discreet Victorian squares built round
a small park of overgrown buddleia and balding grass.

When his key clicked I lost heart. I suddenly knew the rest:
a teenage daughter he was endlessly patient with; his wife
a lawyer or banker; his turn to cook, a bottle chilling, music,
Montiverdi say, or glamrock from his daughter's room.

He'd sleep the sleep of the impervious. Break in, stand
at the end of his bed to proclaim a litany of the world's
nameless and he'd dream on; press a lit cigarette
to his instep and he wouldn't as much as twitch.

I could shake his wife awake but she'd not hear me out.
Before she called the police I'd take the option of leaving.
As she showed me the door I'd tell her not to worry,
in the morning it would be as if I'd never existed.

## Allotment

Through the window you trace out the plot
from the corner to the shop, maybe further,
and cause soil and weeds to settle on tarmac
with the manure you had delivered one weekend,
and dug in the next.

The shed is under the lamp post. Its door,
you tell me, will need repairing.

I love the words you use:
Pentland, comfrey,
main crop, earlies,
fish and bone.

Measuring your steps along the road, I watch
as you count the brittle seeds
from the boat of your hand into the earth
– four at a time, four inches apart.
They are the colour of sycamore wings,
and flat, like lentils.

Afterwards, we leave
and the rich earth becomes street again
– unturned potatoes below the tarmac,
white as eggs.

## Lovesongs

I have never met
the cat we are searching for,
but I feel the loss her name carves
as we sieve this dark field for light

reflected in familiar eyes;
for a cat unable to hear the
ear-twitch and shell-curled sleeping
in the minor third her name makes.

I remember the evening I slipped
you my own shining words of love
and how, later, I watched
as you stood in your kitchen

singing your love back
to the radio.

## Grasshopper Warbler
*BTO ring: J593979*

We opened your wings to count the feathers,
to note how each overlapped the last;
and they held the light like a paper fan,
like a hand of cards inviting the air:
*Here, take one.  Don't tell me what it is.*
*Now place it in the pack.*

This evening, as you run your coded message
out across the Fen, your call unwinds
like a fishing reel,
like a freewheeling bicycle:
*Pick a number.  Don't tell me.*
*Keep it in your head.*

*Mara Bergman*

## The Summer My Father Died

Boys stoned frogs the summer my father died,
surrounded the stream, there was never any hope,
and followed the floating white bellies.

My sister and I were left there, in Accord, New York,
in a bungalow swarming with cousins.
We wanted to be like them, unaware

of our steps as we ran through the dark grass.
Or of night's enormity-all those beautiful stars
forgotten above the wooden roofs.

Our aunts lived windows apart
and our uncles wore those white undershirts
with the scooped-out neck and arms.

On porch steps, as the orange light collected moths,
Aunt Dorothy kissed us goodbye, unable to answer
questions we couldn't ask.

At home, lilacs and roses still bloomed under my window.
Nose pressed against the screen, I longed to hear
my parents' voices murmuring in the garden.

Mara Bergman

## A Quarter to Eight, New York Time

A quarter to eight and the sun streaming in.
      In my life across the Atlantic, the day half gone already,

my children having lunch, the light a little stronger.
      Here, I have no children, husband, house, no work

to go to. I wear jeans ripped at the knees, my hair's unruly
      and I'm for ever dreaming of someplace better.

On my shelf is an oversize paperback, *Vagabonding in America.*
      I read it every night, sleep in an orange mummy bag

I haven't yet shared, my windows open to the whistle of trains
      heading west. I plan to cram my possessions

into the bicycle panniers I made from a Frostline kit
      and cross America with a friend I haven't yet fallen in love with,

who won't be the one to leave me on a corner in New York City.
      That rush of cars up the road in the rain

is always with me. Seventeen and full of hope,
      heading somewhere.

## Gift Horse

She must have been a present
from someone looking up my mother
who didn't know I wasn't one for dolls.

I extracted my games from sagging furry creatures,
not stiff plastic corpses whose look of permanent
surprise had been too much for them.

I would take their clothes off to check
I wasn't missing something worth looking at
and then they would lie around facing backwards,

a memento of someone I'd never known
yet had thanked, kissed and despised
for not bringing a better present.

How long these offerings stayed was down to when
the threat of 'getting together more often' had subsided
and my mother could dispose of them to more grateful children.

I do not know how this one got left,
perhaps losing her leg made her harder to home.
The black smudged ink marks round the hole,

give away how I prized it free with a biro
fascinated to see the shadow
of my finger tips through her mould,

disappointed to find that she was empty.

## Works of Fiction

Pressing my head on the mirror just gives me
an ice cream headache and a view of my skin
where the make up has missed, not a
glimpse, even a breeze from a parallel world.

I don't find auto cues on labels
instructing me to drink, only lists of ingredients,
bar codes, kilojoules. But I can go
where houses don't fit and rabbits run round
like speaking clocks, in dreams switched on
by late night cheese and indigestion.

And emptying wardrobes to check for doors in the back
is one of those jobs I keep putting off,
like defrosting the fridge or cleaning the oven.

Anyway I don't know if I could fit
reversing winter for a lion's kingdom,
into half days already booked
with a hair appointment and a dental check up.

I've never needed such conjuring tricks
to enter kingdoms within my eyes.
It's like playing dress up in your mother's clothes
your own clothes still tugging underneath.

Futures, I rehearse inside my skin
while loading the check out with cat food tins,
ready meals and fair trade bananas.

And conversations past their sell by date
I replay with hind sight words,
as everyday life niggles by like grit in a pearl.

If this was the stuff of fairy tales
Cinderella would settle for just the ball
replaying as her foot slips in and out of a shoe,
and Rapunzel would let down her hair
for neither witch nor prince,
remaining transfixed, by her own split ends.

## Have You Ever Tricked The Cat?

Have you ever tricked the cat
into letting prey drop from its mouth
by pretending nonchalance
then making a grab
at something no more than fear and feathers?

And given the choice between the cat or you,
it throws itself at everything else
hoping that might give way,
and dives into holes too small to hide it.

And you want to say as you pick it up
'I won't hurt you,'
but when you speak you are all the predators
its mother and genes warned about,

and the stroke that reassures the tame
nearly stops its heart.
In the dark of your hand you believe it's calmed
until you see that eye
looking back through your fingers.

That's how it was.
My heart beating as if I ran
and his hand fluttering,
over my hair, my face, my neck, down
below my throat.

It was dark,
but I could not look at him.

## Pond Life

*One black fish among the orange*
*will take the bad luck from the house*

So we bring home a black speckled koi
to add to our eight red-gold shubunkin
*chuchen-cin, kingyo*
that flicker life into the pool.
But our eyes are drawn to the black
packed with its load of ill-fortune.

How can it take in so much?
River soaked up, night sky and fields;
this one absorbs and absorbs;
lightning rod, healed wound,
coal dense as the anchor of black
in Matisse's Snail- its weight
makes the red fish more red, night sky
lit with blue, house bright as fortune.

# Bread

The field of grain the wind blows through.
The bowl of flour and salt made hollow.

The risen dough which fills the bowl.
The proven dough which holds its shape.

The good loaf baked which knocked rings true.
The good loaf cut which makes the meal.

The field of rye the water swells.
The field of wheat or corn made gold.

The loaf we break, the crust and middle.
The wafer on the tongue we take.

The grain, the water and the salt,
the bread we eat, the thirst we slake.

## Albino Blackbird

The truth is, it was only part white;
the bird that came to your garden
two winters ago- but into my head
comes this ghost, shadowless
a white absence, blind negative

in the snow. No reflection glides
over the lake where he flies, light and boneless,
no sound from his throat.

And though you say they never survive, the rare
or different, destroyed by their own kind
I see how he speeds out of the distance,
gathers weight and darkens over the miles
till he meets his own blackness, grows

into lustre; *blackbryd, ouzel, merle*
who quickens the heart a she sings
each night from our gate-post;
his mouth's open crocus, his eye ringed with gold.

## A Frog He Would

'All I want is an omelette,' my father used to say
while my mother was cooking a gourmet meal.
*Psyllophryne didactyla,* the world's smallest frog
hides in debris on the forest floor in Brazil.
'Nothing you do surprises me,' my father said,
which is why I have never resisted a challenge.

I have crouched in cold rushing water
to catch the mating dance of a *Hylodes asper*
while his future mate hops onto my leg
as if it were a rock.  I saw them jump
into the water together, legs entwined,
to reach their particular heaven.

According to Aristophanes, frogs chorused like this:
*Brekekekex koax koax.*
Their mating songs specify what kind of animal
they are, what kind of mate they are seeking -
just like the personal ads.  Females prefer big strong males
and choose a bass rather than a tenor.

The male midwife toad attracts the females
so he can wear their strings of eggs like beads
in a rosary, around his thighs and heels.
Before my sister and I were born,
our parents would punt on the Thames,
its soupy water running between my mother's fingers.

**Dry**
*for Mourid Barghouti*

The poet came from a dry place.
He drank glass after glass of water
when he read in his native tongue,
knowing he must return
to where flesh dries out like fruit.

I thought of the way water splashes,
the trill it makes in a metal cup,
or how it ploughs a path in dust
when it spurts from a broken pipe.

I will remember that when I am thirsty.

## Childcare in the Slaughteryard


Knacker Brown, her grandfather,
fed her on sights and smells
and little presents of boiled meat
hauled clean from the seething broth.

In winter, when the carcasses
lay cold on the sloping flags,
the boiler house breathed warmth;
the fierce walls of the vats,
thick with their years-old grease,
rose into wreaths of steam.
Drawn by their dangerous heat
she edged carefully between them,
hearing the comfortable bubbling
she feared to see when lifted tall.

She grew up close-acquainted
with blood's many lovely reds
and the sequence of its thickening:
an opalescent stripiness that seeped
in rivulets and slowed to form
flat  pads of solid-seeming matter:
rubbery, perhaps possible to peel
and lift? She prodded with her toe;
never touched with fingertips.

Her hands stroked and stroked
smooth quiet necks, so slack,
deep knife-slits almost sealed.
The bleeding done.

*Pauline Keith*

## A Good Ratter

*Aye, she were that.* Every year
at Christmas or the New Year's table
the black cat was remembered.
*Not quite as quick as me, mind.*

*We was watching the same hole* .
My grandfather would pause,
point at the gun-rest on the wall,
look round to check no eye had glazed.

*On the third night - full moon - I got it.*
*She must've been there in the shadow.*
*I shot her paw off with the one same bullet.*
*Biggest bloody rat I ever saw!*

The story ended there. No one ever asked
what happened to the cat. In early dreams
she lurched alone across the cobblestones,
lay down, licked at her shattered stump

while I searched and gathered bits of fur,
picked up splintered bone, found
pads enough, with claws that caught
the moonlight. She let me mend her.

Year on year, the tale re-trumpeted,
I watched her grow - till she crouched,
black panther, by the big rat's hole, eyes
fixed on my grandfather. She sprang.

## Fly Agaric

You took us to the forest,
taught me about nature -
and I learnt well.
Another Sunday visit,
now that you'd left us
and gone to live with her.

Josephine had her hair piled up,
wore silky clothes,
had a nice accent -
didn't hardly use it with us.
She didn't know what to say,
and I don't blame her.

You asked us to chop logs.
My sister grew a rash, fast.
It was mercury, mercury poisoning
from those treated trees.
Mum said you should've known
about the risk, you being a nurse.

My sister recovered, after a few days
in isolation. But we never saw the logs.
Our meals were in the cold kitchen,
those orange-red tiles tart on our toes.
You and Josephine ate in the lounge
in front of the fire.

That day, I forked the peas,
flicked them, forkful after forkful
up the white kitchen wall.
I made my sister tread her peas
into the pale swirls of the stair carpet.
I knew I'd taught you something.

The poison had set in long ago,
through those seven years
of you being my father.
Though you'd taught me to appreciate
the beauty of red and white fungus
and what it could do.

## The Slow Train

The red ink skated on the script, after that call. I was aware only of a low sound made by some animal near my desk, and people gathering, my boss looking at me. Through mountains of air, I was talking, explaining in a voice that wasn't mine. My boss held me, which I knew went against our workplace's code of conduct, but how good her touch felt.

I went to stand and the carpet squares surfed in sequence. Mary walked me to the tube. The ticket barrier was all arms and legs. Mary had her hand, awkward, on my arm, from Brixton to Victoria. She bought us both brandies, and saw me onto the Margate train. I cried solidly. Only one man glanced at me. I was an actor in a film he'd seen before.

I went straight to her. She reached for me from the sheet's constraints. She mouthed my name. It took four years.

## Altar

I find myself still, in the company
of rain and the slow buttery dance
of candlelight. Outside the wind
is a sea longing for a smooth flat shore.

You told me the waves offered
you a watch and once you found
a tiny white cross in stones.

I kiss the secret that made you,
your voice like snow falling
on a dark place.
I kneel in front of your lost altar
and open my hands for the small change
from angels' pockets.

## Memory

With your small hands
you lift the sculpted waves
of the ocean to your cheek
smooth as an olive.
Water whispers in the cave of
your ear hollowed down
to low strings. You close
your eyes, listen to the heart
beat of the sea, a sound
you will remember when loss
gathers your breath and holds it.

## The Rabbits of Skomer

I could lie in your voice,
float in it, drift out to sea,
hang off your soft vowel
sounds, make a hammock
in between the way you
pronounce rabbit, ra-bet.
I could stretch myself out
in the bluebelled grass
of your island, watch puffins
strut around on their sturdy
feet, rabbits frolic without fear
of fox or dog and let   s be honest
even if you're small, fat and bald,
you can have me, just say it again,
ra-bet, my li-tel ra-bet.

## Apple Blossom

*Don't go* my mother said
standing under the apple blossom
wearing that long baggy cardigan
snagged and pilled like a neglected paddock.

How could we not go?
I was doing a last round of the house
checking for something forgotten
but in reality saying farewell.

The removal men had gone.
I looked out of the wash house window
and there she was, unchanged
after twenty years.

The spring before I started school
she had shown me the alphabet
under the apple tree - pale petals fell on the paper
as she traced the shapes with her self taught hand.

Years later I was reading my own books.
In the evenings she banged out campaigning letters,
the old manual typewriter resounding to the clack
of rage and the rasping roller of frustration.

Now my last sight of her will always be
under the apple tree -
*Don't go* she said.

**Fall**

The beech tree is aground, the leaves' stomata
brush the road, bark rusts over harpoons
of barbed wire and roots still suck soil
and stones.  I can see into its heart,
its secret record of peace and war.

It reminds me

of the whale in the museum
rendered to the grandeur of its bones
suspended from the roof, filling the room,
and I leaned from the gallery and touched
the stiff fronds which once sifted the sea's krill.

*Mary Robinson*

## Tape measure

*In memory of my maternal grandfather*

A half moon headstone
and a green bolster.
No photograph
but I see you
in your workroom
the tape looped
round your shoulders
when everything
was made
to measure.

You lived
on the ragged edge
of the village - tailors
always soft or worse -
with cats
and a stray cur.
Catching mice
in a home-made trap
and releasing them
to a nightly reel
of garden
and return.

You died too soon.
I cannot measure
the distance
between us
but I hear you say
*Off the peg*
*from places*
*I only knew*
*on the school room globe.*

32

My mother
had your tape
but not your gift
for making.
Parachute silk
never metamorphosed
into slips
and nightgowns,
the sewing machine
stayed locked
in its wooden ark,
the key
strung on the handle.

After her death
I found
among her sewing things
shoved in an old biscuit tin
with spools of thread
tangled like fishing nets
wrecked by a storm,

that fading ribbon
of yards and inches
each end tipped
with a metal tag
like a thumb nail's
half moon.

## Welsh-English Dictionary
*[Table of mutations]*

When preceded by a d,
the m
mutates into an f,
which is pronounced v.

When preceded by a shop,
the leaving
mutates into a farewell,
which is pronounced ta-da.

When preceded by a shearer,
the sheep
mutates into a shiver,
which is pronounced shorn.

When preceded by a mew,
the red kite's fork
mutates into a fan,
which is pronounced buzzard.

When preceded by a sou'westerly,
the earth
mutates into the Irish sea,
which is pronounced inundation.

When preceded by a pigeon-fancier,
the peregrine falcon
mutates into carrion,
which is pronounced dead.

When preceded by a coal-face,
the man
mutates into a case,
which is pronounced pneumoconiosis.

When preceded by winter,
the black mountain
mutates into a white rhino,
which is pronounced wonderful.

## Anniversary

Some things fatigue faster than others.
It took ten years for the handle
of this coal shovel to begin to flex,
fifty for my left knee to stop,
ten days for these reading glasses
to become unhinged. And us,
by rights rusty as old nails,
still unoxidised. Have I been white zinc
clinging to your iron all this time,
improbably galvanised at St Pancras
Town Hall with the Red Flag flying?
You in your Mary Quant and just two witnesses,
late because they thought we were joking,
causing a queue to build up outside.
Was it 1960's inconsequential hip?
Remember the till on a trestle table:
'You may kiss the bride that'll be five pounds'
- our church bell, our starting call.

## Two Women at Miami International

The final hundred yards.
Your hand gloves mine,
I become colossal,
legs articulated to support
a superhuman weight.

A man stared at us
all through the last half-hour,
as if trying to count our breasts.
I leaned my face to you
put my fingers through
the armholes in your t-shirt.

The digital clock
has guzzled minutes,
it sits bloated
in the departure lounge
vying to outgrow me.

I'm planning the next seconds -
how I will kiss you,
your glasses in your fist,
each glance
full of hours.

**Ashes**

Half of him is in a carrier-bag above the gardening books.
The rest is in the tide, a herring gull's stomach,
or slapped onto the keel of a Brixham trawler.
He's in amongst the whiting as they make for Margate,
dotted on snap-shots of Foster's foot-bridge
strung between St Paul's and the new Tate.

We launched him in a cardboard boat, without permission,
headlong into choppy waves. March gusts whirled
the fine grit under my collar, up my nose. I sneezed
and brushed my coat. Too close, as when, adrift and frail
he thought I was my mother, pulling back the sheet
*Aren't you coming to bed now? Aren't you getting in?*

Below, the Northern Line chuntered to London Bridge
as he'd done every day for forty years. He'd have liked
the gallery café, sniffed at the Rothko retrospective,
travelled sedately in the lift. Then, leaning on my arm
with raised stick heralding the way, we'd have wandered
through the installation in the Turbine Room -

a vast sun caught in its descent, a mirrored ceiling
under which hundreds of people lay in stars or clumps
waving at their reflections through the dust.

**Witness**

6.45 a.m. A parked white Transit
is not Immigration. Abdul answers the door.
*Everyone's asleep.* I tuck myself into the couch,
wonder how we'll stall the dawn.

In Nazaneen and Sahar's Christmas cards
Byron Wood Primary has said farewell.
Sataish's new toy-kitchen back in the box,
no food bought since last week.

We wait. Should get a removal date,
flight-time but no-one's sure.
The MP says *Go quietly*. Nothing
since last week when they came at 8.

The First Line buses ricochet
down Burngreave Road. Microwave pings open.
Shukriya brings spiced tea and almonds.
UK. 2006. So far, so good.

# When She Ran

When she ran all the way from home
to St John, St Michael and All Angels
that April Sunday in her surplice
with no breakfast and her shoes
half-laced, her parents fast asleep
her bright blue cassock flapping
her head already full of
*Morning Has Broken*
and the boy who stood behind her
in the choir stalls whose name
she'd pencilled in her hymn book
and who'd taught her to say *Balls!*
past The Duke of Kendal, Albion Electrics
and The Chocolate Box
she did not know that she was late,
that the nave was full, mid-service
that she would stand baffled at the door
watching the other choristers
processing to the altar,
she did not know her parents
could forget to turn clocks forward,
did not see their lives slip by,
the route past the vicarage
she'd take for Paddington Station
and university, she did not see herself
at 24, wondering if the church hall
would do for her mum's funeral
she did not see herself turning her back,
knowing none of this
was the right time or place.

## Fruitless

My relatives all preach.
We were sent on beach missions,
red and white uniform.
We flexed our limbs,
we had the sun on our backs.
We played Murderball,
my staved nose set itself.
A little girl at Rossnowlagh
pleaded, her Grandmother
reassured her: but sweetheart,
you're already saved.

# Comparison of a Black Labrador with a Sikka Deer Skull

Nose to nose -
indeed, they both seem almost all nose -
those quill curl passageways
wondering back to a plump brain-place;

I shuggled the deer skull
by its sugar-cone tines and he startled
as if those slack teeth could still function.

That week I walked the dog, I thought
he is like the nightmare baby in the attic
that you have forgotten to feed

but he forgives you
in a clumsy pirouette of himself
when you fetch his lead

he has no problem in being too literal,
literal is all he is
meandering the line between skull plates
carrying a ridiculous stick home in his mouth.

## Sonnet of the Noctuoid Moth

*After 'Auditory encoding during the last moment of a moth's life'\**

I have been granted 3 conditions,
all referring to the predatory bat:
*no-bat,          far-bat,*
*near-bat.* I have been given ears
to listen, to hear the no-bat, far-bat,
near-bat. Each ear has two cells,
and possibly a third, vestigial one.
I am allowed what they are calling
anti-bat manoeuvres - auditory moments -
          evasive flight -
before my death. In real life,
before my death, the situation
may be more erratic, beautifully
          pointless

*Fullard, J. et. al. 2003. Journal of Experimental Biology, 206: 281-294*